Bodybuilders

small group bible resources

Relationship building

growing a caring and
committed community

Lance Pierson

Scripture Union, 207–209 Queensway, Bletchley, MK2 2EB, England.
Email:info@scriptureunion.org.uk
www.scriptureunion.org.uk

Scripture Union Australia, Locked Bag 2, Central Coast Business Centre, NSW 2252

Small Group Resources, 1 Hilton Place, Harehills, Leeds, LS8 4HE

Note: *Relationship Building* was originally published under the title *Are You Together?*

ISBN 1 85999 582 9

British Library Cataloguing-in-Publication Data
A catalogue record for this book is available from the British Library.

Cover design by David Lund Design
Internal page design by David Lund Design
Internal page layout by Mac Style Ltd, Scarborough, N. Yorkshire

Printed and bound in Great Britain by Ebenezer Baylis & Son Ltd, The Trinity Press, London Road, Worcester WR5 2JH

Introducing Bodybuilders

ORIGINS AND APPROACH

BODYBUILDERS resources have a strong emphasis on building relationships, helping groups discover the real meaning of **koinonia** – the loving fellowship of Christian believers within which people really care for one another. Group members are encouraged to apply God's Word in ways that produce action and change – all within a secure, supportive atmosphere.

This relational approach to small group experience was first developed in the US by author Lyman Coleman under the title *Serendipity*. In the 1980s Scripture Union, in partnership with another publisher, *Small Group Resources*, took that as the foundation of nine studies under the *Serendipity* branding specially written for the UK market.

This **BODYBUILDERS** series recognises the value and strength of the *Serendipity* approach and contains much of the original material. In a sense, homegroups of the early 21st century may be far more ready to adopt this relational approach than their predecessors. Home groups have moved on; expectations have changed. Revisions and extra new material reflect that progress and also make the series pioneering in the sense of providing a more complete off-the-shelf package.

Christians are not immune from the pressures of society – stresses in the home, workplace, college, places of social interaction. When questioned, most people admit to a deep need for security, a sense of belonging, and a safe environment in which to share themselves and be given support. Many are dissatisfied with the superficial relationships that often characterise contemporary living. They identify lonely chasms in their inner beings, empty of meaningful relationships. They long for practical ways in which to work out their heart commitment to Jesus Christ.

Central to the approach is an understanding that satisfying relationships can be nurtured in small groups in dynamic ways when people are prepared to take risks in opening themselves up to God and to each other. This shared vulnerability works within four contexts:

- **storytelling**
- **affirmation**
- **goal setting**
- **koinonia**

People need to share themselves and need to hear others sharing their own lives for relationships to grow. This is **storytelling**. Everyone needs to be listened to. When we respond to someone with a 'thank you', or 'I found your contribution helpful', we demonstrate that they are valuable and have a contribution to make to the growth of others. This is **affirmation**. Experiencing this in a group that meets regularly – even over a limited time – people begin to share their deeper longings or hurts, discovering that they can trust others for support in their struggles. Individuals can listen for what God is saying to them and implement changes – **goal setting** within the security of **koinonia**. **BODYBUILDERS** encourage all these stages to be reached through Bible study.

MEETING NEEDS IN CHURCHES AND COMMUNITIES

BODYBUILDERS aim to meet:

- **the need for applied biblical knowledge** – Christians are crying out for help in applying their faith in a confusingly complex world. Knowing what the Bible says isn't enough; people want to know how to translate knowledge into action.
- **the need to belong** – increasing pressures, accelerating pace of life, constant change: these work against committed relationships, which many feel should be a distinctive feature of the local church as it witnesses to a lonely generation.
- **the need to share the burden** – pressures on Christians are often intolerable, as demonstrated by emotional/psychological disorders, increasing divorce rates, and the problems of ineffective parenting. One answer is for Christians to take seriously the sharing of each others' burdens – not only prayerfully but practically.
- **the need to build the church as community** – there is a growing conviction that the church should be a community living out the true nature of God's kingdom, experiencing New Testament koinonia.

BODYBUILDERS IN PRACTICE

Using BODYBUILDERS to form new groups: The ideal size for a group is between five and 12, meeting in a home or a church. Newcomers can be added into the group at any time, but care should be taken to give them a thorough briefing on 'the story so far'. The particular purposes of the group in growing relationships and discovering how to apply Bible truths to everyday life need to be made plain.

Using BODYBUILDERS in established groups: This material differs from much on the market to resource small groups. Make sure from the outset that the group appreciates that it is more interactive and, in some ways, more demanding. There is an emphasis on application as well as understanding.

Leading the BODYBUILDERS group: If belonging to this group can be demanding, leading it is more so! The leader needs to have thought about the **BODYBUILDERS** approach and the goals. Ideally, there needs to be knowledge of the group, too, so that the material can be adapted to meet their particular needs. Options are given, and it is the leader who decides which and how much of that material is appropriate. Bearing in mind the emphasis on relationship building, the leader must ensure the group does not become a 'clique', too inward-looking or isolated. The leader makes sure everyone has a chance to speak, assisting those who find contributing difficult. He or she may need to take the initiative in promoting relationship building, which might include practical things like providing lists of telephone numbers, encouraging lift sharing, even organising a baby-sitting rota, as well as exercising pastoral care and leadership.

Each group member needs to feel committed to building relationships and willing to share personally. Regular attendance is a priority. Members aim to make themselves available to each other. Make sure everyone knows that there is complete confidentiality in respect of all that is shared. Encourage prayer for each other between meetings – and set an example yourself.

Practically speaking, you will need plenty of pens and large sheets of plain paper, and sometimes supplies of felt-tip pens, scissors, glue and old magazines or newspapers. Some Icebreakers need pre-prepared visual aids, or even some re-arrangement of furniture! Look ahead to plan for the coming sessions.

All the booklets in this series, each self-contained, contain material for six sessions. Some groups may want to add an introductory evening to explain the **BODYBUILDERS** approach, perhaps in a social setting over a pot-luck meal. The material can be worked through at a slower pace, if that is preferred.

Most of the interactive material is confined to a double-page spread for each session, so that the leader can photocopy it as an A4 sheet to be given out. Alternatively, everyone can have their own copy of the book. Make sure you allow people enough time to jot down answers on their response sheets. Ring the changes: sometimes it's helpful for people to complete responses in twos or threes, especially when a little discussion time is appropriate.

Variety and freedom are hallmarks of the **BODYBUILDERS** material. Leaders can select from the material to put together each session's programme:

Prayer/ Worship (variable time) – options are given, so that you can tailor your selection to whatever your group feels most comfortable with. Hymns and songs suggested are drawn from several popular collections currently on the market published by Kingsway: various editions of *Songs and Hymns of Fellowship,*

New Songs & Stoneleigh, Spring Harvest Praise and *The Source.* Your group may be more comfortable with songs from other traditions. It is always helpful, though, to try to match songs to the theme.

Icebreaker (15 minutes) – this warm-up session is intended to relax the group and focus them on being together, and is usually based on the theme.

Relational Bible study (15 minutes) – this is an initial, fairly light excursion into the Bible verses, relating them to the lives of those in the group through multiple choice questions. If the group is large or time is limited, it may be that not everyone shares every question. By the way, Bible verses quoted in **BODYBUILDERS** almost always come from the NIV (New International Version), but you can use another translation. Often it's helpful to have a selection of different translations to compare when studying a particular passage.

In Depth (20 minutes) – moving deeper into the Bible verses, discovering more about their relationship to life.

My story (10–20 minutes) – an encouragement for people to relate teaching to everyday lives.

Going further (15 minutes) – this often involves other parts of the Bible containing similar teaching. If not used during group time, this can be taken away for further personal study during the week.

Enjoy! Discover! Grow!

BODYBUILDERS
small group Bible resources

Growing through change – seizing the opportunities life gives you
Lance Pierson

Do we fear change because we have mis-placed our emotional security? These six sessions challenge you and your group to find security in God himself, to welcome any kind of change as an opportunity to deepen that trust, and to discover strength and support in the community of the church.
ISBN 1 85999 585 7

Designed for great things – wrestling with human nature
Anton Baumohl

Human beings – beautiful and unique yet rebellious and capable of evil! Only the Christian view of man makes real sense of the good and bad things about being human. These six sessions will help you and your group to discover your true potential in Christ.
ISBN 1 85999 585 3

Living for the King – growing God's rule in our world
'Tricia Williams

'God in control? It doesn't look like it!' Is that your reaction to the suffering and injustice you see in the world? These six sessions look at key issues which have immediate relevance for those who want to be involved in the risky and exciting business of being God's community here and now.
ISBN 1 85999 584 5

Surviving under pressure – finding strength in the tough times
Christopher Griffiths & Stephen Hathway

We live in high-pressure days, bombarded with conflicting views and influences that can be obstacles to adopting lifestyles that truly reflect Christian values and principles. These six sessions are aimed at equipping Christian believers to stand firm even on the roughest ground.
ISBN 1 85999 585 X

A Fresh Encounter – meeting the real Jesus
David Bolster

Some were intrigued, attracted to him, accepted, loved and followed him; others were afraid of him, were disturbed by him or rejected him. These six sessions challenge you and your group to extend your understanding of who Jesus is and what that means in everyday life.
ISBN 1 85999 586 1

Available from all good Christian bookshops or from Scripture Union Mail Order:
PO Box 5148, Milton Keynes MLO, MK2 2YX, Tel: 01908 856006
or online through www.scriptureunion.org.uk

RELATIONSHIP BUILDING
– growing a caring and committed community

INTRO

It is impossible to live daily life without constant interaction with other people. At the most superficial level, there are the people we rub shoulders with – neighbours, the friends we say 'hello' to in the street or on the bus, shop assistants, the person who stops us to ask the way or the time. In addition, many of us share our homes with family or friends, and our day with workmates or children. Each interaction expresses a relationship, and carries potential to develop and deepen it.

These relationships are not simply an accidental fact of life; they are a psychological and emotional need. Unless we have people to talk to, to touch, to share with, we shrivel and wither instead of blossoming and growing. *God sets the lonely in families* (Psalm 68:6) – indeed, he planned for all of us to be born in them – because we need each other.

If this is true of the human race as a whole, it is no less true of God's new community, the church.

A previous generation (in which some of us may have received our Christian upbringing) emphasised personal piety – the individual's relationship with God – to the virtual exclusion of fellowship – our relationship with each other within the Christian community. We have now rightly come to see this as a distortion of Jesus' intention. Alongside the great

commandments, *Love the Lord your God*, and *Love your neighbour as yourself*, he added a new commandment, *Love one another. As I have loved you, so you must love one another* (John 13:34). The healthy hunger for right relationship with our fellow Christians has created the prolific growth of small fellowship groups, such as the one in which you will be using this book. In small groups of four to twelve we can learn the art of giving and receiving love. And unless we learn that, we shall get nowhere as disciples. Jesus himself set the pattern with a small group of twelve.

The sessions focus on a variety of relationships both inside and outside the church:

1. Belonging together – relationships with those who brought us up
2. Living together – relationships with the opposite sex
3. Growing up together – relationships with children
4. Bind us together – relationships within our church
5. Getting back together – relationships under strain
6. You've got it together – using affirmation to keep relationships in good repair.

Each session focuses on our relationships with particular people, draws on skills needed to build and develop the relationships and, within the caring atmosphere of the group, initiates practical action to put the skills to use.

BELONGING TOGETHER

AIM: to focus on relationships with our family and to share what things (both positive and negative!) each group member has inherited from his or her background in terms of upbringing and faith.

NOTES FOR LEADERS
People often do not realise how deeply they are influenced by their formative years, both physically and spiritually. Often these are positive parts of God's providence, and this session in no way tries to disturb group members' feelings about their past. It aims to give people a chance to talk about their social and spiritual roots. This is an extremely valuable stage of group-building, so encourage an open, trusting atmosphere (perhaps by taking the lead in sharing some of your own answers). For many people, however, their experiences of family life are *not* positive ones and some of their memories may be painful. You will need to be very sensitive to that and it would be best to err on the side of leaving people free not to share their answers publicly in this first session if they would prefer not to.

PRAYER/WORSHIP IDEAS

Worship
If this is a first meeting for the group, encourage members to be free to express themselves in worship in ways they find meaningful and to be accepting of the way others may choose to worship. Make clear that clapping or raising hands or arms, etc are acceptable (indeed, biblical!), as are different postures for prayer (kneeling, sitting, standing, etc). If you have a musician in your group, ask them (in advance!) to come prepared to lead a time of sung worship. If you're without a musician, using a CD and providing the words for people

to sing along is just as good. Use songs today which help you focus on being in the family of God and the transformation he can effect in us:

Father God, I wonder
Jesus put this song into our hearts
Lord, I come to you
Our confidence is in the Lord
I will change your name

At the end of the meeting
Read 2 Timothy 1:6,7. If there are any folk in your group who have identified things during the meeting which they feel are hindrances to them living an effective Christian life or witnessing boldly to others, gather round and lay hands on them as Paul did to Timothy. Pray that they will be filled with God's Spirit and have a new sense of the power, love and self-discipline that he brings. Over the coming weeks, continue to exhort each other to fan into flame that gift of God.

ICEBREAKER
Demonstrate how this works by showing your shield as you introduce it. The motto may require more thought; give some typical examples: eg 'Blood is thicker than water', 'Do it or die trying' or even something more light-hearted. When they are ready, ask people to show their family crests in twos or threes.

BIBLE READING
Acts 16:1–3; 2 Timothy 1:5–7; 3:14–17

RELATIONAL BIBLE STUDY
Suggest that people stay in their small groupings – pairs or threes – for sharing throughout the rest of this session. For this study, encourage them to share not just the factual answers, but the memories they evoke.

IN DEPTH

MY STORY

If your time is short, Question 1 may work better as something for people to do at home after the session. Question 2 enables people to talk more fully with one or two partners about their spiritual beginnings; it is immensely valuable to forming relationships, but you may feel that people have done enough 'baring their souls' for the first session. Question 3 (again limited to the people who have been sharing together throughout the session) is an important

conclusion to the proceedings; when people have talked about themselves it is reassuring to learn that others have found it helpful.

GOING FURTHER

Question 2 is the safety valve in this session for negative experiences of background. Pray for the supportive, healing dimension of your fellowship together; and do everything you can to encourage relationships of complete openness and confidence within the group.

notes on the Bible verses

 Acts 16:1–3; 2 Timothy 1:5–7; 3:14–17

It seems probable that Timothy became a Christian on Paul's first missionary visit to Lystra. He immediately became one of Paul's closest companions travelling as Paul's representative to Thessalonica (1 Thessalonians 3:2,6) and Corinth (1 Corinthians 4:17) and staying on as Paul's delegate in Ephesus (1 Timothy 1:3) to establish the young church there. Here it was that he received the two personal letters preserved in the New Testament; the second is probably the last letter on record written by Paul.

Acts 16:1–3 The implication of the Greek phrasing is that Timothy's father had not been a Christian and was by now dead. In time, Paul became like a replacement father to him.

16:2 Good reputation among fellow Christians is an indispensable qualification for leadership (compare 1 Timothy 3:7,10,13).

16:3 Many Jews would have regarded Timothy as an illegitimate half-caste because of his mixed parentage. His circumcision now was to remove unnecessary obstacles to evangelising the Jews.

2 Timothy 1:5
Paul's emphasis on 'reminding' draws Timothy's attention to his family and spiritual roots, and

the reassurance they can provide in times of testing.

1:6 Paul (and the elders) laid hands on Timothy when they commissioned him to join the missionary team (see also 1 Timothy 4:14). It was then that he received the spiritual gift necessary to serve God. To remain alight and available to God, our spiritual fires need constant fuelling and stoking.

1:7 Timothy was young and inexperienced. His father had probably not provided him with an

adult example of a male Christian (if the deduction from Acts 16:1 above is correct). These two factors, put together, may help explain his natural timidity. Paul instructs the Corinthians not to take advantage of Timothy's timidity, in 1 Corinthians 16:10,11.

3:16 'God-breathed' is the exact translation of Paul's word; it implies that God controlled the Bible's composition to ensure that it contains and communicates what he wants. 'Teaching, rebuking' and 'correcting and training' are probably two pairs of positive and negative opposites, the first referring to what we believe, the second to how we live.

9

BELONGING TOGETHER

ICEBREAKER

In the shield below, fill in your family 'coat of arms'. In each quarter you must write or draw something which expresses an aspect of your family which is important to you. For example you might draw your mum or dad on one, write a quality you have inherited from your mum in another, draw a favourite memory of a family holiday in another and draw the family pet in the last one. On the band at the top, write your family 'motto' – this might express in a few words the chief outlook on life that you were brought up to hold. Explain your family crest to the other members of the group.

BIBLE READING

Acts 16:1–3; 2 Timothy 1:5–7; 3:14–17

RELATIONAL BIBLE STUDY

1 Timothy's father and mother came from different races and religions (Acts 16:1). My parents differed in (circle any letters that apply):

a nationality
b the part of the country they came from
c religious beliefs
d political views
e ideas on how to bring up children

f value of money
g sense of humour
h leisure activities
i other _____

Beside any that you have circled, draw one of these faces to express the effect their differences had on you: I enjoyed the variety [smiley face]; It didn't matter to me [normal face]; It made me feel confused/insecure that my loyalties were split [confused/unhappy face].

2 Who was the chief source of *sincere Christian faith* (2 Timothy 1:5) in your home or family?

a no one
b grandparent
c mother
d father

e brother/sister
f you
g other _____

IN DEPTH

1 What belief/value of your home upbringing do you most strongly agree with?

2 If Paul took me on a missionary journey, I would be good at working with (tick any that apply):

a children
b teenagers
c men
d women

e old people
f immigrants
g ill or handicapped people
h other

Put a cross against any you would not find it easy to work with. Is there anything in your home background that you think might influence your strongest tick and cross?

3 Timothy's chief weakness was *timidity* which God was working to overcome with *a spirit of power, of love and of self-discipline* (1:7). Re-write this verse to identify the greatest weakness you have inherited from your background and to suggest how God wants to build you up to overcome it.

God did not give me a spirit of _____

but a spirit of _____

4 How are you most aware of God using the Bible in your life (3:15–17)?

a Making me wise for salvation
b Teaching me
c Rebuking me
d Correcting me

e Training me in righteousness
f Equipping me for every good work.
g Other _____
h I'm not aware of God using the Bible in my life

MY STORY

1 On the back of this sheet write a short thank-you letter to someone who was involved in influencing you positively as you grew up, to express gratitude for the best things you gained from them. This might be a parent, relation, friend, youth group leader, teacher, etc.

2 Jot down brief notes to help you tell the one or two others in your small group how your faith first 'became sincere', or came alive. Share your 'story' when your group leader gives you the opportunity.

going further

1 Discuss how the following features of Timothy's background could have been disadvantageous to him:
a One parent a Christian, the other not.
b Mother and grandmother Christians but not father. How can we be of spiritual help to children with this same background today?

2 Think back over your childhood and teen years. Think particularly about difficult times, unhappy incidents, bad memories. Do any of these remain with you today – unresolved? Share any of these if it will help and if you are able to, with your group or with an individual in your group. If you prefer not to talk about them, offer them to God and seek his continued help and healing.

LIVING TOGETHER

AIM: To focus on our relationships with the opposite sex; to celebrate God's creation of the human race as male and female; and to develop sensitivity to the other group members' attitudes to sexuality.

NOTES FOR LEADERS

British people, especially Christians, tend to find it difficult to discuss sex. There are some safeguards in the way we have constructed this session; but again, do not force people to share their more personal answers if they do not want to. The session is not about marriage, although married couples should benefit from it incidentally; its aim is more to develop sensitivity to the sexual nature and needs in all of us, especially the unmarried.

PRAYER/WORSHIP IDEAS

Songs and hymns

Choose songs which focus on relating, one to another, in God's family, and on God's healing power:

Jesus stand among us
Rejoice, rejoice!
Say the Word
O God of grace (how good it is)

Prayer

Remember that the Lord God said *It is not good for the man to be alone* (Genesis 2:18). One of the positive things about being in a small group is knowing that we do not have to struggle through life alone. You might like to spend some time supporting the members of your group in prayer for any practical needs, or issues which may have come out of the My Story section.

ICEBREAKER

A task similar to Adam's in Genesis 2:19,20! Start with people sharing in clusters of three or four which animal character they most identify with.

BIBLE READING

Genesis 1:26–31; 2:18–25

RELATIONAL BIBLE STUDY

Questions 1 and 2: If women find it impossible to imagine themselves as Adam (Question 1) or men as Eve (Question 2), ask them to answer the question as if they were the man or woman they know best (husband/wife, father/mother, boyfriend/girlfriend).

IN DEPTH

MY STORY

Question 1 – Again, assure the group that no one is required to share their answers with anyone other than God. However, many people may well find it helpful to talk further with someone sympathetic; either yourself or other pastoral carers within your church. Question 2 can also be answered alone and followed with silent prayer; but it offers the chance to open up further sharing within the group. Your fellowship will deepen, the more you can thank each other and ask for each other's help like this.

GOING FURTHER

Things to remember ...

notes on the Bible verses

 Genesis 1:26–31; 2:18–25

There are profound truths about human nature to think over here.

1:26,27 The words *image* and *likeness* were design terms taken from the building trade. 'Men were placed on earth as God the ruler's statue' (Von Rad), that is, the human body is God's construct for revealing his glory. 'God looks at us and sees a reflection of himself' (Luther). There are many ways in which we reflect him, but the two specified here are: a) active, responsible stewardship of the earth's resources (1:26); b) the two sexes, expressing different sides of his character and outgoing love. (This passage is explored more fully in another BODYBUILDERS booklet: *Designed for Great Things;* Session 2.)

1:28–31 The writer introduces these two activities of sex and work as part of God's blessing on the human race; not, as so many have assumed, part of his curse.

2:18,20 *Suitable helper* in English may make the woman sound subordinate to the man. But the Hebrew word is never used in the Old Testament of an inferior; indeed, sixteen times it refers to a superior! Here God assigns the woman equal partnership with the man through the word 'suitable', which means 'corresponding to' or 'one who perfectly complements'.

2:19,20 In naming the animals, Adam exercises initiative and discernment, fulfilling the role God designed for him.

2: 21–23 Unlike the animals, woman is made of the same stuff as the man; he even shares his name with her. (Hebrew for 'woman' sounds similar to 'man'.) Marriage is designed to include this sensation of *reunion* with 'my other half' – 'we were made for each other'.

2:24 *Being united* includes every level of a married couple's sharing; one home, one family, one 'bank account' (?) as well as one bed. *Becoming one flesh* stresses their sexual union as the expression and reinforcement of their commitment to each other.

LIVING TOGETHER

ICEBREAKER
Which of these animals do you see yourself as being most like? Why?

BIBLE READING
Genesis 1:26–31; 2:18–25

RELATIONAL BIBLE STUDY
1 If you'd been Adam what would you have said when God introduced Eve to you (2:33)?

a Excuse me, this is a 'men only' club!
b The kitchen's behind the fig tree.
c Darling, we were made for each other!
d Well, I suppose she's better than a
rhinoceros.

e Just what I've been looking for!
f Where have you been all my life?
g Other _____

2 If you had been Eve, what would have been your first words to Adam?

a Well, it's a good job I'm here. You'd never have managed to subdue the earth on your own.
b Only Adam? Bit boring isn't it?
c Isn't it great? We'll be able to work at this together!
d Just a point, dear: God did say 'helper', not 'drudge'.
e I know my place – your needs are more important than mine.
f I think the tigers would be tamed more easily than you.
g I've written out my side of the agreement; you sign here!
h Other _____

IN DEPTH
1 What impression do you get of God's attitude to sex?

a We don't talk about it.
b Naughty but nice.
c Strictly for procreational purposes!
d Very good.

e What you do when you're in love.
f What you do only if you're married.
g Disgusting!
h Other _____

2 Tick which of these qualities you would think it essential to share with a marriage partner. Then grade them in order of importance:

nationality
social background
intellectual ability
respect for each other
sense of belonging (to each other)

political views
religious faith/philosophy of life
attitude to children
sexual attraction
Other _____

food likes/dislikes
spare time interests
being in love with each other
similar age

MY STORY

I You will NOT be asked to share your answers to this question with anyone else in the group! But God is, of course, interested in how you feel and would like you to share it with him. Draw one of these faces alongside each aspect listed below of how you cope in living with yourself:

[happy face]   I feel comfortable and am happy with God's provision.
[unsure face]   Not sure. Ask me again sometime.
[sad face]   I don't cope very well and need God's help.

a When I am on my own I feel …
b About my sexuality (maleness/femaleness) I feel …
c About my body I feel …
d About my 'marital state' (married/single) I feel …
e About my relationships with the other sex I feel …
f About my relationships with my own sex I feel …
g About close friendships I feel …

2 This group (or some members of it) could best help me get myself together in the areas of need this session has focused on, by (tick the way you think would be most helpful):

a praying regularly for me.
b letting me talk things over.
c showing me they love me as I am.

d encouraging me to spend more time with my spouse/family/friends.
e minding their own business.
f other _____

going further

I How far is marriage breakdown always attributable to failure in one or more of the three processes in 2:24?
a leave father and mother
b be united to spouse
c become one flesh

2 If God says, It is not good for man to be alone (2:18), why does he leave so many people single for so long? How can we help them, especially if they wish they were married?

3 How would you answer people who say the following:
a 'There's nothing wrong with sleeping with any consenting adult, provided you love each other.'
b 'You should keep sex for someone you're going to live with faithfully, but there is no need to get married.'

GROWING UP TOGETHER

AIM: To focus on your relationships with children; to appreciate the high value Jesus sets on childhood; and to encourage the growth of childlike qualities in each other.

NOTES FOR LEADERS

'In order to know a person truly, you need to see them with children' (Margaret Evening, *Who Walk Alone*, Hodder & Stoughton 1974, p153). This session is primarily about how we relate to children and to the child who still lives in each one of us. The focus isn't particularly on members of the group who are parents of young children; though naturally they will both greatly benefit from and contribute to it. If some people find 'childhood' too big a period for simple answers, suggest they pinpoint the age of eight or nine.
If group members find it difficult to see the relevance of a study on childhood, remind them of the special place Jesus gave to children in relation to the kingdom.

PRAYER/WORSHIP IDEAS

Songs and hymns
Spend some time focusing on our relationship to God our Father and the simplicity of worship that he desires:

I'm your child
The Father's song
As for me and my house
This is my desire
When the music fades (the heart of worship)

Prayer
Have some balloons available. Give one to each member and, as they blow it up, ask them to think of a child whom they know and would like to pray for. You might like to write the child's name on the balloon and display them all in the middle of the room. Spend a few minutes describing the children and then pray for them together. Take your balloon home to remind you to pray for that child during the week.

ICEBREAKER
List some of your childhood favourites, and start re-living some of these memories:
my favourite childhood game:
my favourite childhood pet (or animal in the zoo):
my favourite childhood hiding place (or place to play):
my favourite childhood adult (other than parents):

Share answers in small groups of three or four at the most. Encourage people to talk about the feelings these memories recall; you will have difficulty stopping them!

BIBLE READING
Matthew 11:25–27; 18:1–6, 10–14; 19:13–15; 21:14–16

RELATIONAL BIBLE STUDY

IN DEPTH

MY STORY
Encourage people to take time to reflect deeply on these questions. Questions 1 and 2 – share answers as a basis to praying for each other. You may want to leave question 3 without sharing; but it will be enormously enriching if you feel you are committed enough to each other to share your response and to lay hands on each individual and pray for them. Be open to listening to God here. He might want to give you some specific words of encouragement to share with people.

GOING FURTHER
Be sure to pass on to your church leadership any criticisms or suggestions that emerge from this discussion.

notes on the Bible verses

**Matthew 11:25–27;
18:1–6, 10–14; 19:13–15;
21:14–16**

Jesus was no starry-eyed sentimentalist over what children are really like. He was well aware that they can be sulky and unco-operative (Matthew 11: 16,17). But the collection of passages chosen for study summarise his positive teachings about the value of children and childhood. It is a higher view than anyone else has ever put forward, investing children with innate dignity. Each passage reverses one or another popular assessment of children in Jesus' age and ours.

11:25–27 The paradox here is that children are open to God's revelation, while *the wise and learned* (the official experts, Pharisees and law-teachers) are not. *These things*, which children perceive (11:25), seem to refer back to the miracle earlier in the chapter which disclosed Jesus' identity as Messiah (11:3–5, 20–23); and forward to the personal knowledge of God which Jesus his Son mediates (11:27). As throughout these passages, Jesus uses the term 'children' (25) to illustrate a spiritual condition (11:27).

18:1–5 The child of verse 2 becomes a visual aid for three startling truths:

a childlikeness is necessary to enter God's kingdom in the first place (18:3);
b childlikeness is the secret of spiritual greatness (18:1,4)
c Jesus challenges us to treat children with the same love and respect we would give him (18:5).

Jesus described the child in front of him as being 'humble' – he was 'nothing' in the eyes of the world: no status, property, money; rather, he was completely dependent on his parents to provide all that he needed.

18:6,10–14 With graphic pictorial language Jesus stresses God's vigilance in protecting the smallest and weakest in his flock.

a He warns off those who would corrupt them (18:6) – *a large millstone* was pulled by an animal, as opposed to the portable kitchen variety;
b They are very close to his heart. He always has them in view (18:10).
c He personally searches for any who wander away (18:12).

19:13–15 The disciples may not have been anti-children as such, they may simply have thought that Jesus was too preoccupied with his approach to Jerusalem to be delayed. If so, he retorts that he is NEVER too busy for children; they have the right of direct access to his blessing at all times. More than this, he gives them the charter of citizenship in heaven. Indeed, THEY are the archetypal members who show others the way to enter; see 18:3,4 for further exploration of this claim.

21:14–16 The temple authorities were shocked at the lack of ritual purity (the Pharisees usually excluded the blind and lame from the precinct because of their deformity) and of dignity – fancy allowing children to go on carolling bits of the pilgrim psalm AFTER the procession had finished! Jesus hits back at them with a double-edged quotation from Psalm 8:2.

a It is genuine praise that reaches God, not hypocritical or insincere praise no matter now 'unofficial' the worshippers may be.
b Implicit in the second half of Psalm 8:2, which Jesus leaves unspoken, is the charge that the temple authorities have become God's enemies.

GROWING UP TOGETHER

BIBLE READING
Matthew 11:25–27; 18:1–6, 10–14; 19:13–15; 21:14–16

RELATIONAL BIBLE STUDY
1 How do you react to Jesus' attitude to children? (Circle any letters that apply.)

a He'd have made a marvellous father.

b He obviously never had any kids of his own!

c He must be talking about 'spiritual children'.

d He's biased against adults.

e He's too sentimental.

f Other _____

2 Mark A (agree), D (disagree) or P (perhaps), to express your reaction to these common opinions about children:

a Children should be seen and not heard.

b Little angels ...

c Spare the rod and spoil the child.

d School days are the happiest days of your life.

Tick any that you think Jesus would agree with; put a cross by any you think he would disagree with; put a question mark next to any you're not sure about.

IN DEPTH
1 You're having an enjoyable chat with another adult, when a child comes to ask you a favour. What would you usually do?

a Ignore him and hope he'll go away.

b Make him wait until you've finished your conversation.

c Smile sweetly but inwardly resent the interruption.

d Welcome him as if he were Jesus (18:5).

e Other _____

2 How can we humble ourselves like children (18:4)?

a Let other people sit in the best chairs or have the biggest bit of cake.

b Enter our second childhood.

c Say we're no good at anything.

d Never push ourselves forward.

e Rely on other people for everything we need.

f Trust God without question.

g Other _____

3 What childlike qualities do those people have who belong to the kingdom of heaven (19:14)?

a Innocence

b Knowing they're weak and small

c Spontaneous directness

d Being happy to do what God says because he says so
e Trusting God to keep his promises
f Soon forgetting grudges
g Accepting gifts joyfully
h Excitability
i Awe and wonder at God's love for you
j Lack of self-confident sophistication
k Knowing you need help
l Other _____

MY STORY

1 *Your Father in heaven is not willing that any of these little ones should be lost* (18:14). One way I could help to care better for the children who belong to us in this group/church is ...

_____
_____

2 Now focus on one 'child in your life', whom God has made you aware of during this session. It may be a close relation (child, grandchild, nephew, sister, etc); or a child you have some other special relationship with (godchild, someone you teach, neighbour, penfriend, etc).
Through this child, Jesus wants to teach me ...

_____
_____

To treat this child more like Jesus would (18:5), I need to ...

_____
_____
_____
_____
_____

3 To the 'child' in me (the part of me that is childlike and may, in some respects, still be childish), Jesus is wanting to ... (Circle the letter that comes closest to what you sense Jesus is feeling for you now; if you know any further detail fill it in on the lines):

a reveal something

_____

b call me to *stand in the midst* while he teaches the others something through me

_____

c say, *You are the greatest in the kingdom of heaven*

_____

d give assurance that I can't stray too far for him to reach me

_____

e shout that he's coming to find me

_____

f place his hands on me and pray for me

_____

g say, 'I love your praise'

_____

h Other

_____

going further 〰️

1 How might we, even inadvertently, fall into the danger of causing children to sin (18:6)?
2 How effective is your church's pastoral care for children or older young people who appear to lose interest in God (18:12)?
3 What bearing, if any, do 19:13–15 and 21:15,16 have on the age and conditions for baptising children and welcoming them to Communion?
4 In the light of his teaching in these passages, what more could your church family be doing to nurture its children?

BIND US TOGETHER

AIM: To focus on your relationships within your own church fellowship; and to explore the family togetherness Jesus intends for his people.

NOTES FOR LEADERS
This session explicitly attempts to deepen relationships among your group members. In particular, it aims to widen the focus to include relationships with others in your church family. The main method used is affirmation.

PRAYER/WORSHIP IDEAS

Songs and hymns
Choose songs which help you to focus on God's purposes for his people:

For I'm building a people of power
Father of creation
Great is the darkness
I will offer up my life

Prayer
Set aside some time during the evening to pray for those who have given up something in order to serve God, either in this country or abroad. This might take the form of praying for particular missionaries or part/full-time workers in the local community who are supported by your church. Alternatively, contact a mission agency who would be glad to supply you with some guidelines for prayer.

ICEBREAKER
You have 10 minutes for the group in small teams to build a church with the highest possible tower, all out of newspaper and sellotape. The highest free-standing tower at the end of the time, wins.

You will need to provide lots of newspaper, Sellotape and scissors for this activity. Encourage the group to talk together about church as they build. What are some of the positive things that they perceive about their church, ie the love people have for one another, a heart for the poor, etc. Are there some things they could continue to work on as a body?

BIBLE READING
Mark 3:20, 21; 31–35; 10:28–31
RELATIONAL BIBLE STUDY

IN DEPTH
Question 4: This is the most direct and personal form of affirmation in that each member names who they see as most gifted by God in different aspects of discipleship. It runs the risk that some people may not get named at all. If you feel that your group is not yet ready to share this level of openness in the full circle, ask people to compare answers in pairs.

MY STORY
Questions 2 and 3: Either decide in advance whether to focus these questions on the group itself, or on the wider church fellowship; or let each member choose for themselves. Question 3: Do everything you can to give each member what they ask for as soon as possible – preferably on the spot!

GOING FURTHER

Things to remember ...

notes on the Bible verses

Mark 3:31-35; 10:28-31

Without mentioning the word 'church', these passages hint at the 'family' basis of the Christian church.

3:31,32 Jesus' mother and brothers did not at this stage understand his mission at all, and had come to take him away (see 3:21). They expected their natural family relationship to have first claim on Jesus' obedience.

3:33–35 But he responds that there is an even deeper obedience to pay (to God's will), and an even deeper family relationship among those committed to it.

10:28 Peter compares the band of apostles favourably with the rich man who has just left Jesus, unable to give up his possessions (10:21,22).

10:29,30 Jesus underscores the truth that God will let none of his disciples lose out even in this life. But he reminds them that this life is the age of persecutions; we shall only experience the promised blessings in their fullness in the age to come.

10:31 And he prevents any jockeying for position, reward or most favoured status, with the reminder that God's valuation often reverses our expectations.

BIND US TOGETHER

BIBLE READING
Mark 3:20,21; 31–35; 10:28–31

RELATIONAL BIBLE STUDY
I If Jesus had been your son/brother, what would you have done? (Circle any letters that apply.)

a Been proud to have a preacher in the family.
b Shrugged it off, hoping he would get over it later.
c Gone inside and made a scene.
d Told him he was no longer welcome at home.
e Gone to see your doctor/minister.
f Joined the circle around him.
g Suggested he made an appointment with a psychoanalyst.
h Followed him around each day with a packed lunch ready.
i Other _____

2 In which areas of your life do you feel you are like Jesus' natural family – standing outside the house where he is staying, feeling a bit estranged from him? In which areas of your life do you feel more like those he called his true family – sitting at his feet, learning from him, and doing God's will?

Put a cross somewhere on the line next to each category, to show which group of people you identify with most closely.

	Right next to Jesus	At the back of the room	Outside	Down the road
In my family relationships, I'm ...				
In my main occupation/work, I'm ...				
In my use of money, I'm ...				
In my use of spare time, I'm ...				
In my church commitments, I'm ...				

IN DEPTH
I What are you conscious of having 'left' to follow Jesus?

a everything   **e** independence
b home   **f** ambitions/career
c family   **g** nothing
d healthy bank balance   **h** other _____

2 What does Jesus mean (verses 29,30) by receiving *a hundred times as much*?

a We're better off as Christians than we would be otherwise.
b We are compensated at least a hundredfold for everything we give up.

c The blessings outweigh the sacrifices beyond any comparison.

d We feel all experiences (persecutions as well as gifts) much more intensely than before we were Christians.

e Relationships within the church family can be even deeper and give an even greater sense of belonging than relationships in our natural families.

f Other _____

3 See 10:29. Apart from any member of your natural family, who or what in your church fellowship comes closest to giving you the emotional support of:

home (security) _____   father _____

brother _____   child _____

sister _____   'fields' (responsibility/work to do) _____

mother _____

4 Who in this group have you come to see as making the following contributions to the 'family' of your group?

open home _____   using livelihood in God's service _____

brotherliness _____   enduring persecution/suffering _____

parental care _____   childlikeness _____

making us aware of eternal spiritual realities _____

MY STORY

1 One good thing I have received from belonging to this church is ...

_____

2 One good thing I have received from belonging to this group is ...

_____

3 One way we could express our family-togetherness more closely in this church/group is...

_____

4 One thing I would like this church/group to give me (eg more support/encouragement, a chance to play in the music group, a chance to talk) is ...

_____

going further 〰

1 How can we help those suffering tensions because the lifestyle and values of their natural family are different from those of their church family?

2 What form, if any, does persecution for Jesus and the gospel take for you? Are there points at which you avoid persecution by going too softly? If so, what should you do about them?

3 What obstacles are there to your church being a more close-knit spiritual family? How could you overcome them?

GETTING BACK TOGETHER

AIM: To focus on any relationships under strain; and to explore how to repair them.

NOTES FOR LEADERS

Before the session, decide very carefully which sections you plan to include; if In Depth Bible Study, prepare a separate slip of paper for each person.

PRAYER/WORSHIP IDEAS

Songs and hymns

Choose songs that help you to focus on Jesus and his power to unite and heal:

Jesus, stand among us
Bind us together
What a friend we have in Jesus
Meekness and majesty
Purify my heart
Jesus be the Centre

Prayer

You might like to pray together about the issues raised in the My Story part of the session. The group should pray specifically for each other and you could start the next session with a progress report if appropriate.

ICEBREAKER

Groups of three will work equally well; simply omit the Avoider. Let the 'family row' run for about five minutes, then call a halt. Ask people to discuss what the conflict felt like, and how far the Peacemaker succeeded in resolving it. How close was the group members' experience?

BIBLE READING

Genesis 32:3–21; 33:1–12.
Before reading the set passage, fill in the background by referring to the first paragraph of the notes on the opposite page.

RELATIONAL BIBLE STUDY

Question 1 will look something like this:

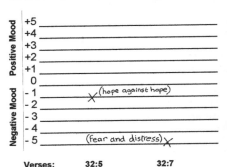

| Verses: | 32:5 | 32:7 |

IN DEPTH

Sharing of answers is entirely up to the individual. It gives a chance for group members to hand over to God any sore relationships among each other. It is especially suitable if you are in the practice of sharing Communion together as a group. But it needs sensitive handling and if you do not feel confident about it you would do better to replace it with one of the study passages in Going Further.
Question 3: Collect the slips of paper, place them on a baking tray and set fire to them in full sight of the group. As you do so, assure them that God forgives our sins, removes any barrier to peace between us, accepts our tokens of repentance, and fills us with his love for each other. Perhaps accompany the flames with a reading of a few Bible verses, such as Hebrews 12:28,29; Psalm 103:12; Ephesians 2:13–18; 2 Corinthians 7:9–11; 1 John 1:6,7; 3:14.
Question 4: Structure this as is most appropriate for your group. If you are celebrating the Lord's Supper, it will be a natural part of the worship. You may suggest members use a formal greeting to each other ('The peace of the Lord be with you'), or you may prefer a more informal mingling and sharing of news and needs. Or it might work better as a

session of prayer for each other. The section of the Bible passage which suggested this response is 33:4; your group may be able to express love through an embrace, but never attempt to force this if it is not natural. Similarly, it may be appropriate to suggest that people use this opportunity to apologise privately for way they have offended other members of the group, and/or to give their real or token peace-offerings. It may be more helpful for them to go away and do this outside of the meeting however. But do stress that **it is only helpful to confess to 'visible' sins of word or deed**; we're not wanting people to start dredging up every little ill-feeling. Going around admitting bitter thoughts towards unknowing victims usually just stirs up further recriminations!

MY STORY

This is a good example of goal-setting. Each member should focus on the relationship in their life most in need of repair, and then on what practical step they could take to help make peace within the next few days.

GOING FURTHER

Things to remember ...

notes on the Bible verses

Genesis 32:3–21; 33:1–12

The background to the story is this. Esau and Jacob were twins, but at odds with each other from birth, largely because of personality and parental favouritism (25:25–28). Although he was the younger twin, Jacob had cheated Esau of the birthright (25:29–34) reserved especially for the eldest, and of their father's blessing (27:1–40). Esau vowed to kill him, so Jacob fled to his Uncle Laban in Haran, 500 miles away (27:41–44). He stayed there at least fourteen years (29:16–30), till God told him to go home (31:3). And that meant facing Esau.

32:12 Jacob reinforces his prayer with God's own words. The command in verse 9 quotes 31:3; and this verse claims God's promise in 28:13–15.

33:3 Sevenfold bowing was a sign of homage paid to a king.

33:10 Comparing the sight of Esau's face to God's would, on its own, be a vivid compliment to his brother's free forgiveness, and recognition of God's activity in answering his prayer. But in the full context it is also the echo and achievement of Jacob's mysterious overnight wrestling-match with God (32:24–30).

GETTING BACK TOGETHER

ICEBREAKER

Form groups of four. Take on the roles of a family living together: mother, father, two children. (It doesn't matter if you have to play the part of someone of the other sex.) Now give each member of the family a different one of these personality types:
• Attacker – accuses and blames the others for everything.
• Avoider – tries to get out of every responsibility he/she can.
• Martyr – always ends up doing someone else's dirty work.
• Peace-maker – the only mature one of the four, seeking to resolve the conflict justly and harmoniously (not necessarily one of the parents).
Scenario: Mother points out that everyone has left dirty washing-up on the side, despite an agreement last week that you would all do your share. Let things run from there!

BIBLE READING
Genesis 32:3–21; 33:1–12

RELATIONAL BIBLE STUDY

1 Draw a mood graph to record Jacob's emotional ups and downs through this story. Put one word/phrase alongside each point you plot to sum up how you think he was feeling then.

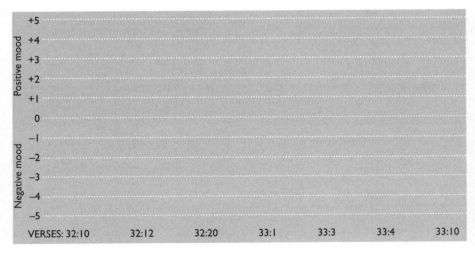

2 The time I most felt like ...
Jacob in 32:7–11 was _____
Esau in 33:4–9 was _____
Jacob in 33:10,11 was _____

IN DEPTH

Your answers to the following questions are initially for your own use. There will be an opportunity to share answers, but only those (if any) that you wish to.

1 Is there any member of this group I feel I have...

a misjudged
b thought unkindly of
c envied
d felt threatened by
e got heated with
f argued against unnecessarily
g talked unkindly about
h mistreated in any other way

2 Remember Jacob's peace-offerings (32:13–21)! What present would you give, if you could, to help make it up to any person/people listed in question 1?

PERSON   PRESENT

_____   _____

_____   _____

_____   _____

3 On a separate slip of paper, write what you would like to give and say to that person (or to God), in order to make peace. The paper need only be seen by God; it will be offered to him and burnt.

4 Commit each other to God's peace.

MY STORY

1 The person I am most conscious of not being fully at peace with is my:

a brother/sister.
b spouse.
c parent/child.
d neighbour.
e colleague/work-mate.
f boss/assistant.
g friend.
h fellow-Christian.
i other _____

2 Compared with Jacob and Esau's relationship we are at the stage of:

a falling out.
b being miles apart.
c being out of touch.
d God telling me to go back.
e thinking about peace offerings.
f making first steps towards each other.
g embracing and making up.
h trying to rebuild.
i other _____

3 What I need to do, in order to move on to the next stage in our relationship, is:

_____

_____

going further

1 For Jesus' teaching on the activities in this session, read Matthew 5:21–26.

2 For a short, New Testament example of conflict and reconciliation, follow the story of Paul and Mark in Acts 12:25; 13:13; 15:36–40; Philemon 23,24; Colossians 4:10; 2 Timothy 4:9–13.

3 For a longer New Testament case study of damaged relationships under repair, read 2 Corinthians (with the help of a commentary), especially 1:1–2:4; 6:11–13; 7:2–16; 10:1–11:21; 12:11–13:10. Discuss what light these passages throw on your understanding of this topic.

4 For a study of the qualities required to be a peace-maker within the Christian fellowship, read Ephesians 4:2,3,15, 25–32. Discuss how these qualities exist in your group/church fellowship.

YOU'VE GOT IT TOGETHER

AIM: To focus on your relationships with this group; and to leave them in first-class working order at the end of this course through practice in giving affirmation.

NOTES FOR LEADERS

Don't forget at some stage to ask for progress reports on the peace-making goals people set for themselves at the end of Session 5.

This session brings the course to a close and will hopefully give people an opportunity to sum up what it has meant to them and end with prayerful, committed support for each member as they set personal goals.

PRAYER/WORSHIP IDEAS

Songs and hymns
Choose songs which express confidence in and worship to God:

O God of love (How good it is)
Our confidence is in the Lord
My Jesus, my Saviour
Jesus, name above all names

You might like to use Psalm 133 as a basis for meditation too.

Prayer
Use the My Story session this evening as the main focus for your prayers. It's a good opportunity to really support your group by praying specifically for them and listening to God for them.

ICEBREAKER
If some people find it hard to affirm qualities, they may also include skills (eg good guitar-player, cake-baker or Bible

study leader). And while they should not repeat words already listed, they may find variants of the same concept (eg kind, generous, self-sacrificing).

BIBLE READING
Philippians 1:3–11

RELATIONAL BIBLE STUDY
Spend no more than 10 minutes on this. As always, the value in sharing these questions will not be the bare answer, but the explanation of it.

IN DEPTH

MY STORY
If you feel it is appropriate you might like to do this as a small act of commissioning. Alternatively, share Communion together. The sequence is as follows:

a One person shares and explains their challenge/need.

b Someone else in the group/sub-group responds by reading the encouraging words of verse 6, if possible expanding and applying it (eg 'Over these last six weeks I have seen God at work making you more patient, and I believe that as he carries on doing this, you will find his resources to cope with …').

c The first person sits in the centre of the circle, and either one person or the whole group lay hands on his/her head and prays the prayer of verses 9–11 aloud, with special reference to any particular need.

GOING FURTHER

notes on the Bible verses

 Philippians 1:3–11

This passage hints that Paul was writing from prison (1:7); later verses make it explicit (13,17). There seems a real possibility that he will be executed (1:20; 2:17). The traditional assumption is that he wrote this while he was awaiting trial in Rome (Acts 28, c. AD 63). In the circumstances, it is all the more remarkable that he starts his letter with praise and prayer, so much more concerned for the Philippians than for himself.

1:5 'Partnership in the gospel' refers both to their collaboration with Paul in founding and extending the Christian community in Philippi 'from the first day' that he arrived there; and to their financial support for his later missionary work elsewhere (4:10,14–18).

1:7 God's grace is his love which we go on experiencing, even in adverse conditions; and the ability he gives us to serve him in all circumstances. Paul adds the further thought that it is sharing God's grace together that produces such strong, almost tangible, love for each other.

1:9–11 The threefold prayer – for love, knowledge (1:9) and righteousness (1:11) – is a perfect general request for spiritual health to use for any Christians, whatever their particular needs.

YOU'VE GOT IT TOGETHER

ICEBREAKER

Everyone should have a large sheet of paper stuck on their back, and a felt-tip pen in their hands. Walk around the room, writing two words on each person's back, to express qualities about them which you appreciate (eg 'mature', 'wise', 'fun', 'kind'). You cannot repeat any word that someone else has used.

When everyone has finished, read your paper and savour it. Which quality do you find most surprising and which are you most pleased about?

BIBLE READING

Philippians 1:3–11

RELATIONAL BIBLE STUDY

In the questions below, use Paul's words to help you express what this group course has meant to you.

1 *Your partnership in the gospel from the first day until now* (1:5). Doing this course together has deepened my commitment to following Jesus …

a not at all
b a little
c a lot
d radically

2 *All of you share in God's grace with me* (1:7). Through doing this course together I've seen that God has blessed me…

a not a lot
b a little
c a lot
d radically

IN DEPTH

1 *I thank my God every time I remember you* (1:3). Who do you remember with thankfulness, and why? It might be someone in the group or outside it.

2 *In all my prayers for all of you, I always pray with joy* (1:4). How can this be a feature of your prayers for people? (You may want to keep the answer to this next bit private.) Is there anyone you *don't* think of with joy? How might this change?

3 *It is right for me to feel this way about all of you, since I have you in my heart* (1:7). My feelings about this group are:

4 *God can testify how I long for all of you with the affection of Christ Jesus* (1:8). What does it mean, in practical terms, to have 'the affection of Christ' for people?

MY STORY

1 At the end of this course, the chief challenge I believe God is setting before me is ... (for instance it might be some responsibility he wants you to take on, some problem to sort out, some need he wants to meet in you or through you).

_____

_____

2 When you have heard each other's challenge or need, encourage each other by reading and applying verse 6: *Be confident of this, that he who began a good work in you will carry it on to completion until the day of Jesus Christ.*

3 Then pray for each other, using the words of verses 9–11.
This is our prayer:
• that your love may abound more and more in knowledge and depth of insight,
• so that you will be able to discern what is best
• and may be pure and blameless until the day of Christ,
• filled with the fruit of righteousness that comes through Jesus Christ
• to the glory and praise of God.

going further

The New Testament is full of affirmation. Paul starts with a resounding affirmation in a number of his letters – see Romans 1:8–15; 1 Corinthians 1:4–9; 1 Thessalonians 1:2–10. In the case of the Corinthians, Paul's first purpose in writing is to rebuke (1:10 – 6:20); but even so he starts by affirming.

Here are some examples of Jesus in action as the Affirmer: Luke 7:9, 24–28, 44–50; 8:48; 10:42; 12:7,32; 18:15,16; 19:9; 21:3,4; 22:15,28–32; 23:43.

So why are we so slow to look for the good in people; to congratulate, compliment and encourage? Think of the things that prevent you, your group, your church, from giving affirmation. Discuss what could help to remove any obstacles you identify.

'Does your Bible study deal with the issues that friends are talking about at the pub or in the office?'

If you want to talk to your friends about why the Bible is relevant to what they are into, these are the Bible studies for you.
Mike Pilavachi, Soul Survivor

A great way to explore up-to-date issues and concerns in the light of the Bible.
Rev Dr Michael Green, Advisor in Evangelism to the Archbishops of Canterbury and York

How can you engage with friends and colleagues as they discuss best-selling novels, chart music, pop culture TV shows or Oscar-nominated films?

CONNECT can help – innovative, creative and thought-provoking Bible studies for groups available as an electronic download or in print.

Titles available

- Billy Elliot
- The Matrix
- Harry Potter
- TV Game Shows
- Chocolat
- How to be Good
- U2: All that you can't leave behind

With more coming soon

Available from all good Christian bookshops
from www.scriptureunion.org.uk
from Scripture Union Mail Order: PO Box 5148, Milton Keynes MLO, MK2 2YX
Tel 01908 856006
or as an electronic download from www.connectbiblestudies.com

connect Bible Studies are jointly produced by Scripture Union, Premier Media Group and Damaris Trust.